*The First Book of the Lamb*

# The First Book
# of the Lamb

Peter C. Stone

Gabriel Press
Ventura, California

*I have yet many things to say to you, but you cannot bear them now. When the Spirit of Truth comes, he will guide you into all the truth; for he will not speak on his own authority, but whatever he hears he will speak, and he will declare to you the things that are to come. He will glorify me, for he will take what is mine and declare it to you.*

—John 16:12-14

# CONTENTS

*And in the last days it shall be, God declares, that I will pour out my Spirit upon all flesh, and your sons and your daughters shall prophesy, and your young men shall see visions, and your old men shall dream dreams . . . .*

—Acts 2:17

# INTRODUCTION

This book may well represent a milestone in the intellectual evolution of mankind. It is an unusual book, presenting an unusual scope of circumstances, experiences, and incredible new insights into the very nature of man and of man's purpose on earth.

Prior to the events recorded herein, my life had been totally devoid of what one might classify as psychic or religious experience. Furthermore, my personal theological credo was simply one of a firm belief in a God and a divine order that were manifested more in the trees, the wind, and the stars than in religious doctrine. I was an ordinary businessman, husband, and father, who would in occasional moments of solitude attempt to make sense of a natural order that somehow, deep within, never really felt right.

Then one day my world turned upside-down. And when it righted, months later, everything had changed.

You will find chronicled herein the first seven months of a spirit visitation that is still in progress today. The experiences described are true, for they actually happened exactly as set forth. Similarly, the information obtained from those experiences is accurately and faithfully recorded without the adulteration of conjecture, personal opinion, or any scientific, theological, or philosophical doctrine.

Simply put, this book truthfully sets forth what happened and what I was told. It is presented here for you to read, to digest, and from which to form the basis of your own opinion. In so doing, I suggest that you diligently consult the footnotes as they appear; they are an essential part of the story to be told and of immense importance in developing the perspective required for an informed judgment.

All biblical references are to the Revised Standard Version (second edition) of the Holy Bible. Where specified, reference is also made to the *Doctrine and Covenants* of the Church of Jesus Christ of Latter-day Saints, the Book of Mormon, and the Koran as translated from the Arabic by J.M. Rodwell (London: J.M. Dent & Sons, Ltd.).

It is for you to decide.

Peter C. Stone
September 26, 1984

*Behold, I am bringing upon you a nation from afar,*
  *O house of Israel,*

                              *says the Lord.*

*It is an enduring nation,*
  *it is an ancient nation,*
*a nation whose language you do not know,*
  *nor can you understand what they say.*

                    —Jeremiah 5:15

# ONE

The date is April 15, 1984. It was just yesterday that he instructed me to begin placing the events and information of the past few months on paper. As I write, I feel his spirit upon me—a now-familiar feeling—guiding every thought and word.

It all *seemed* to start about six years ago. Several years earlier, I had become the unwilling recipient of the attentions of an individual to whom the ruthless, calculated, parasitic extortion of others was a way of life. My family, my reputation, my business, my assets—all had eventually fallen prey to a protracted assault of such a heartless and uncaring nature as to epitomize the very essence of evil.

I seldom prayed in those days, except for an occasional private and internal prayer to my Maker. Although I had been a regular church member for years, I had never been active, nor did I attend but infrequently—and when I did, it often felt *wrong* deep inside. I was religious not in the doctrinal sense, therefore, but rather in some inexpressible, personal, deeply intuitive way that I did not fully understand.

By then the long, unrelenting siege had threatened, destroyed, or tainted virtually everything I held dear; anguished and distraught, I had reached a personal crisis of massive proportions. My family was emotionally decimated, my friends were steadfastly looking the other way, and my mind had become seized with a paralysis that seemed to prohibit all rational thought. I was profoundly desperate, and I no longer knew what to do or to whom to turn.

Therefore, I asked God for help.

I was driving to the office that morning, my mind literally spinning with helplessness. As I drove, the maelstrom within my head quieted for the merest instant, and I began thinking about God—and about how He was now my only hope, since all else had obviously failed. I began to pray within the silence of the automobile. I asked for mercy; I asked for help; and in the event neither were according to His will, I asked to be let *out.*

The result was astonishing. I felt a strange, fleeting sensation at the top of my head; then, a sudden, strong pressure bore down upon my brain as though radiated from above. I quickly drove to the side of the road, braked the car to a stop, and sat motionless for a few moments, somewhat dazed by the totally inexplicable phenomenon I had just experienced.

As I sat by the side of the road with the car engine idling, I became aware of a strange, utterly foreign sensation within my body and brain—a calm self-assurance of a magnitude I had never experienced. I had spent years flailing against my attacker with constant mental turmoil

16

and anguish, and suddenly I was calm. And I knew what to do.

I calmly drove to my office, calmly placed several telephone calls, beginning with my attorney, and calmly watched the situation resolve. My family was so shocked by the sudden change in my personality that it was weeks before they had adjusted to the untroubled husband and father who now came home each evening. Ever since that moment I have been calm and self-assured, and it happened like the flick of a switch.

# TWO

My business is seasonal, educational in nature, and is perceived as somewhat of an institution by the field it serves. It is an emotionally satisfying and financially successful business that allows ample spare time for sailing, a life-long avocation in which I have enjoyed a pleasant and continuing familiarity with the sea.

The business is a source of fulfillment and pleasure for me, for through it I relate to many fine people whose friendship I cherish. During the last few years, however, I had wrestled with increasingly recurrent episodes of a strong, compulsive urge to abandon the business and cruise the world on our sailboat. It was a strange dichotomy of perceptions, for although I knew quite clearly that I would not enjoy such a venture, the compulsive feelings relentlessly developed in both frequency and insistence.

One night last June, I dreamed. Transported by sleep, I found myself walking upon a sidewalk; glancing backward over my shoulder, I could see that it led away from a fenced enclosure that contained a large number of highly functional and utilitarian buildings—an institution of some sort.

As I walked away I became increasingly happy, and free of spirit.

An automobile stopped at the curb, and the driver offered me a ride. An old, trusted friend of many years standing, his invitation sparkled with the lure of an efficient means of placing great distance between myself and the institution. Unsuspecting of his underlying motives, I happily slid into the passenger's seat and was soon engrossed in conversation, oblivious to the route he was taking.

The true nature of his mission suddenly became apparent, however, as the car passed through a gateway and rolled to a stop within the familiar confines of the institution. A few steps beyond the car, a person dressed completely in white patiently awaited my return. Chagrined, I opened the door and stepped out.

The person in white invited me to walk with him, therefore we set out upon a cement sidewalk that skirted the buildings. He walked on my right, his feet occasionally brushing the edge of the manicured lawn of the institution. To my left were the nearby building exteriors; monotonous and utilitarian, they were punctuated with conduits, wires, and pipes that had been painted to match the wall beneath.

As we walked, we discussed my reasons for leaving the institution and his reasons why I should not. The conversation growing in intensity, we stopped behind a building: he standing on the sidewalk and I leaning against the exterior wall of the building, with my left arm resting along the top of a horizontal pipe.

As the debate heated, I began to realize that his right hand was behind his back, hiding something from my view. Suddenly I saw what it was, as it streaked for my left arm and the pipe it rested upon: a huge pipe wrench, perhaps

19

four feet in length, and it had securely clamped my arm to the pipe beneath.

I awoke from one of the most startling dreams of my life, instantly realizing that the full color, vividly detailed images had already become permanently engraved upon my memory. As I lay there, wide awake, I opened my eyes. Two white, luminous, perfectly spherical balls met my gaze, floating just below the ceiling. Maneuvering in a fashion which suggested a lack of mass, they moved about the room for several minutes, hovered briefly over the bed, then suddenly flew northward at high speed, silently disappearing through the bedroom wall.

Needless to say, I was shaken. But I also knew that something very real had happened—something beyond my personal experience and understanding of reality, but nevertheless *real*. And whatever it was wanted me to not abandon my business.

# THREE

The following August, I hauled the boat for some mechanical repair and a long-needed coat of bottom paint. As I worked, my mind began to vacillate indecisively. I thought, "If I *must* get away and the business *must* continue, then the only solution is to acquire a manager who is trusted and true. But who?" And the answer would surface: Paul.

Almost as rapidly as the answer surfaced, however, I found myself discounting it, for although Paul is a wonderful person, I thought to myself, he hasn't the maturity and experience to handle the job well. But who? Perhaps I should just abandon the business? But what about the dream? Perhaps if I could just get someone trusted and true to manage it—how about Paul? Thus the cycle continued, compulsively and without slowing, day after day. The thoughts were so constant that I yearned for a thought on any other subject to break the repetition, but they continued relentlessly.

One afternoon, the tedious cleaning, painting, and repairing had finally neared completion. It was the fifth day in the yard, and as I worked, the thoughts continued to rotate mechanically and wearily within my mind. Always the same problem, always the same untenable solution—Paul—and then always the same problem again, endlessly and unceasingly. A familiar voice stirred the monotony, and I looked up to see my wife entering the boatyard. She was happy and smiling, eager to share the news she had just heard: We were to have company that weekend—Paul and his wife Elizabeth were coming to visit from their home in Arizona!

An amazing coincidence, I thought to myself. I had seen neither Paul nor Elizabeth for months, and a visit was even more rare; why were they coming *this* week? And why had the endlessly circling thoughts that had plagued me for days suddenly vanished? *What was going on?*

I hurriedly packed my tools, drove home, and was soon dialing the telephone. Elizabeth answered, and proceeded to tell the following story:

"Paul has been feeling despondent lately, for his career seems to be heading nowhere. And although I enjoy school, I can now take a Master's rather than continue for the Doctorate, and I find myself also compelled to seek a change. Somehow things just don't seem to be going in the right direction, although everything is just fine above the surface.

"We've both been vacillating strongly this past week, so I thought I'd try to get some help breaking the cycle. I visited for several hours yesterday with one of my professors at school, a good friend of long standing who teaches clinical psychology, is 'into' metaphysics, and is just a very grand and highly perceptive person.

"At any rate, we talked for a long time, wandering from subject to subject. After several hours, he suddenly said,

'Stop—what was that you just said?' I answered that I was just mentioning your business and how both Paul and I absolutely love helping you and your wife in it on occasion. He then said something very unusual: 'I know nothing of this fellow or of his business, but I felt you "light up" when you mentioned it. I'm not sure why I feel this way, but I know that is what you must do—what you must work in. Call him right away to make whatever arrangements you can.'"

Paul and Elizabeth spent the weekend with us, exploring possibilities and renewing our feelings for each other. As we casually shared our recent experiences, however, we began to realize that the uncharacteristic, strong vacillation we had independently experienced several days earlier had occurred simultaneously; it even *felt* the same. We then found that we shared the same eerie sense of somehow having been directed to one another, in some compelling manner almost too subtle to perceive; that, too, had occurred simultaneously. Needless to say, the "coincidences" of the past week became major topics of conversation.

# FOUR

Two months later, I found myself vacillating again: "... abandon the business and go sailing ... don't do it, for you love the business ... abandon it ... don't ..." and so on, as the thoughts circled relentlessly, day and night. Upon discussing the situation with my wife, she assured me she would lovingly do whichever I chose, but I had to *choose.* She also asked, "Why do you want to go sailing?"

That caused me to think, for I had never enjoyed cruising for more than two or three weeks at a time, and I was now considering years at a time. Why? *Why?* Then a strange perception began to form deep within me, something wordless, indescribable—but *something.* After a few more moments of reflection, I said to her, "I don't know why I feel the way I do, nor do I know why I'm perceiving the thing I'm perceiving—but I *am.* I feel, deep down inside, in some inexplicable way of *knowing,* that if I could just submerge myself in the serenity of a long sail over calm seas, or of weeks in a beautiful, calm lagoon—I think if I could do that, that somehow—in some way that I don't understand yet—I would learn the secrets of the universe!"

She looked at me askance and muttered something about how I always seem to accomplish the bizarre things I mention, but that this was indeed a tall order.

But the conviction persisted, strange but real. Day after day, as we discussed what had now become a major dilemma, the same eerie perception would consistently float to the surface of my mind: that in some way I could not quite discern, but nevertheless in a way I knew was true, I would learn the secrets of the universe—if I could just get away!

The compulsive and illogical nature of my conclusion was clearly apparent to both of us, but I nevertheless found myself constantly returning to the same unfathomable perception that I was somehow on the verge of extraordinary knowledge of the basic nature of things. Furthermore, the feeling was so strong that it seemed almost as though I already had this knowledge at some level and just couldn't quite remember it.

This cycle of events repeated for perhaps ten days; then, one evening after dinner, I began to recall the compulsive feelings that preceded Paul and Elizabeth's unexpected visit. Then I remembered the compulsive feelings surrounding the events six years ago, when I called to God for help and instantly received it. I wondered: could these feelings be somehow—*connected?*

I didn't have to wonder long.

The next morning, while driving to the office, the words of a prayer spontaneously formed within my mind. Moments later a feeling of intense immediacy literally propelled the words from my mouth as I stated aloud within the silence of the car: "Dear God, my head is ringing with notions of your Creation—if you really want me to know the secrets of the universe, I'll be only too happy to receive them! And if it is your will that I be given this knowledge, I promise to use it in whatever way you wish, according to your will."

I felt a sense of anticipation as the compulsively circling thoughts of the past few days suddenly slipped from my mind. I went to the office, enjoyed a pleasant day, and returned home in the early evening.

That night, everything changed—forever.

# FIVE

As I walked through the doorway, my wife was comfortably propped on the living room couch; in her hand was a book we had read the previous year concerning metaphysical phenomena. As she began to talk about the material she had been reading, the thought suddenly sprang into my mind, "Why don't we try it now?" The ouija board! I had read of them, of their record of almost total nonperformance, but I had also read of extremely rare instances where they provided very real—howbeit very brief—communication with *someone.* In a moment of compulsion I had purchased one many weeks ago, and it had since been riding about, forgotten, in the trunk of my car.

My wife hesitantly replied, "I don't know—I don't think I'm ready. For some reason, I have a strange feeling, a *knowing,* that things will never again be the same after we take this step."

I persisted gently while maneuvering two chairs such that we could sit facing each other with the board upon our laps. I had read that the only rational communications ever received were after a long wait of perhaps several days, so I prepared for a boring evening. At least, I thought, I have someone lovely to look at.

Within moments of my initial inquiry of "Is anyone there?" the white plastic pointer suddenly burst into action, moving to the *yes* on the board with such alacrity that it almost jumped from our grasp. The communications began immediately, and as the night progressed we found ourselves receiving vast quantities of information from a world—or a reality—that only hours before did not even seem to exist. Each message was carefully spelled, with the pointer meticulously moving from letter to letter as we followed the motion with our hands. Most of the messages dealt with the process of reincarnation, but some were also pleasant stories—delightful, intellectual "fairy tales" that were to begin, as gently as possible, the development of our ultimate understandings.

Thereafter, our unseen visitor (who referred to himself simply as a "consciousness") communicated with us for four to five hours each evening. But as the flush of first excitement waned, I began to wonder to whom—or more specifically to *what*—we were actually speaking. The information was always rich, the personality pleasant, courteous, and righteous—but still I wondered, for I knew I was a blind man in an alien world.

One day, perhaps a week after the initial contact, I found myself pacing our living room, musing on our experiences and worrying about—I didn't know, but *worrying.* I stopped for a moment and picked up our family Bible. We knew it as our family Bible because it had been with us for the past twenty-five years; although, for some unfathomable reason, I had never read it. I had owned it; I had kept it with me wherever I had lived; I had required that my children be well versed in it; but I personally had never read it, other than in an extremely occasional and cursory manner.

Very, very curious, I thought to myself.

I sat down on the couch, arbitrarily parted the pages with my thumb, and opened the Bible to a random passage; a chapter heading attracted my eye, so there I began to read. Seconds later I sat bolt upright, suddenly realizing that, inexplicably, the exact location at which my reading had commenced contained the solution to my greatest concern. For there, in plain language, was the test of the spirits:

> *By this you know the Spirit of God: every spirit which confesses that Jesus Christ has come in the flesh is of God, and every spirit that does not confess Jesus is not of God.*
> (1 John 4:2-3)

Within moments I was back at the board with my wife, with whom I had just shared this new revelation. We excitedly opened the dialogue with our spirit friend and immediately put the question to him: "Do you confess that Jesus Christ has come in the flesh?"

Without hesitation, the pointer moved to a resolute *yes*.

# SIX

As we gained confidence with the board, we became increasingly amazed by the sheer wit, intellectual vigor, and knowledge of our visitor. Each day's session surpassed the former in an exciting, ever-increasing spiral of new information and new concepts regarding life, reincarnation, and the purpose of man's very existence.

But one evening the daily communicative romp suddenly became intensely serious as we somewhat incredulously learned that I had incarnated in the nineteenth century as Joseph Smith and previously as Mohammed. Several days after that astonishing disclosure, our unseen friend then proceeded to render us totally speechless by announcing that my present lifetime was ordained for a very specific and special purpose; that I was someone known as the "Lamb"—and that it was my task to make ready, on earth, for the coming of Christ.

Although we were stunned and dumfounded, our visitor continued without a loss of stride, weaving a grand and cosmic context for the startling pronouncement he had made. Through the medium of the board he spoke of the universe, of creation, of God and His plan, and of the drama beginning to unfold. For several days he continued in this vein, until one morning, our threadbare composure only barely regained, we watched with wide-eyed amazement as the white plastic pointer moved to spell the words: *I am the Holy Ghost.*

Moments later, he announced that it is *he* who is coming as Christ.

He explained that his task now at hand was the redemption of those souls who had successfully learned the lessons that earth and mankind are for. He also revealed many things about himself—not only who he was but who he had *been,* and why. And what his name would be when he comes as Christ.

Then we asked about Satan, and about evil. And our world abruptly turned into a living, breathing hell.

# SEVEN

Once broached, the subject of evil came upon us like a dark storm. Since we possessed such an abundance of knowledge concerning the coming Christ, he explained, we would now be sought out by evil spirits who would try to destroy us.

The effects were subtle at first—small, crawling sensations, like insects moving initially within the brain and then spreading to the abdominal area. He assured us that evil spirits were real and that they had located us, and the evidence of our senses left little doubt that, indeed, they had.

Several sleepless nights later, he gave us a method to protect ourselves from the evil spirits; however, its effectiveness waned after a day or two, whereupon they returned even more aggressive and horrible than before. A subsequent protection method involved violent shaking of the head and the use of repeated incantations; it seemed silly at first, but as the attack progressed in intensity it was the only thing that would keep the internal crawling sensations out of our bodies.

Eventually, the repulsive spirit-things began to develop an apparent immunity to these defenses, and we became increasingly fearful that they would soon overwhelm us. He therefore recommended that we surround ourselves with candles, claiming that they would protect us from the evil spirits—and they did, for a while. Then he said that only *white* candles would work, so I hurriedly acquired some while my wife shook with fear at home.

A day or two later, the pointer unexpectedly ceased its familiar function of spelling messages; although it continued to move in response to questions, the motion was suddenly limited to a brief signal of affirmation. No data— just a simple back-and-forth motion for a *yes,* and nothing more. Miserable and confused, we were huddled on the bed within our protective ring of white candles; outside, a long holiday weekend had just begun. We knew the candles wouldn't last until the stores reopened on Monday. The board no longer functioned, except for the affirmative motion of the pointer, and we could feel the evil spirits beginning to stir within us again. The siege had continued for almost two weeks now, and it was promising to get even worse than ever. Nothing—absolutely nothing—seemed to protect us from the horror we were experiencing. We were sleepless, we were gaunt for fear of leaving the candles to shop for food, and we were powerless to affect our unknown fate.

Suddenly, a strong, exceptionally clear thought shot to the surface of my mind—*Bibles.* Using the board, we asked, "Would Bibles help?" and the affirmative motion of the pointer sent me scurrying to find all the Bibles I could. Needless to say, we were delighted to discover that, when applied to the body, the Bibles totally prevented the crawling, horrible, spirit-things from entering. We finally had a few hours sleep; awakening, however, to the sickening discovery that the things were now developing the capability of entering any area of the body not covered with a Bible. It was beginning again, as horrible and repulsive as ever.

Another intense, extraordinarily distinct thought then appeared within my mind, to the effect that total bodily coverage was required and that a large blanket made from the *pages* of Bibles would work. Using the board, we asked about such a blanket and received an encouraging affirmative response. But where would it end? How could I make a blanket with sufficient strength from the tissue-thin pages of our Bibles? Also, the only relief we had experienced recently was from those Bibles, and we were reluctant to destroy them. Furthermore, my wife was literally trembling with fear; where would I find, on a holiday weekend, enough additional Bibles to make a blanket without driving to town and leaving her for several hours? I knew she wouldn't leave the candles, and I suspected she might not survive if I left her for more than moments.

I stood up within the ring of candles in our bedroom and looked out the window; two young men in dark suits, shined shoes, and fresh haircuts were walking past our home. Suddenly, another crystal-clear thought briefly overwhelmed my mind: *Books of Mormon.* Using the board, now as an almost automatic response to the strong thoughts, I asked, "Would pages from the Book of Mormon work?" The pointer moved affirmatively, leaving my mind spinning in a vain attempt to correlate the information. Choosing my words carefully, I countered, "Do you mean that, like the Bible, it *too* is the Word of God?"

The sheer vigor of the affirmative response galvanized me into action.

I ran outside and accosted two very surprised young men on mission. I was disheveled, gaunt, and crosses were drawn on my body from previous protection methods that no longer functioned. I asked for all the Books of Mormon they had; obligingly, they offered me the two copies they carried in their hands.

A brief word of thanks, and I was back inside the bedroom again, planning a blanket. We asked, "May it be machine sewn?" No answer. "Must it be hand sewn?" The pointer moved in an affirmative response.

We spent the next twenty-four hours hand-stitching a giant blanket, three pages in thickness. We sewed by candlelight, for we had learned a few days earlier that electric lights neutralized the protection of candles. As we labored hour upon hour in the semidarkness, our sore and oft-punctured fingers left telltale spots of blood upon our work.

When we finished, I wrapped my wife in the blanket— and it worked. Finally, it worked. Until two hours later the invisible *things* began crawling in through the imperfectly sewn seams.

Bewildered and exhausted, we lit our entire remaining supply of candles for extra light and restitched every seam of the gigantic blanket. It took every last ounce of energy and every last candle. I wrapped my wife again, and she immediately fell into a deep sleep.

I walked outside the ring of sputtering candles and decided to take a quick shower. "When they pick me up with the white coats and straitjackets, I may as well be clean," I thought wryly. I was strangely controlled and calm, considering the state of affairs.

As I showered, I pondered the events of the past several weeks in a seemingly hopeless attempt to understand our circumstances; then, unexpectedly, my thoughts coalesced into a clear perception that began to dance and celebrate within my mind. After a moment's reflection I said aloud within the shower stall: "Dear God, I don't know why you are doing this to us, but I do know one thing: No matter what you do to me or my wife, I still *know* he is who he says he is. I know deep within that he is the Holy Ghost and the Christ and *nothing* will change my mind."

I left the shower, donned a bathrobe, and walked into the bedroom. My wife had just awakened. She smiled and said, "They're gone; I don't feel a thing!"

And she was right—it was over. I had passed my test.

# EIGHT

That night we ecstatically received an absolutely incredible and thoroughly delightful barrage of information. The messages continued to be mental, with the extraordinarily clear words and phrases rising effortlessly within my mind. Continuing the procedure that had been thrust upon me over the past few days, I would verify each message by repeating it aloud, with affirmation signalled by a simple, restrained, and almost regal back-and-forth motion of the pointer.

I soon found that I could also ask questions and verify messages by merely *thinking* the words, rather than speaking them, with the pointer continuing to respond as though the words had been voiced aloud.

We were told more of the wonders of creation, of God and His plan, and of my role as Lamb for the coming Christ. As we conversed in this manner, however, I began to notice a new sensation: I could feel an electric tingling within my back, on the upper right-hand side—a pulsating sensation—and it was synchronized with the pointer movement!

As the secrets of the ages flowed to us throughout the night, the pulsating sensation in my back became stronger and stronger until it was almost overwhelming. Suddenly, I realized what new wonder had occurred: he had established a *totally internal* communicative protocol. As the messages appeared within my mind I could now verify them mentally, with the strong, electric, pulsating sensation signalling his affirmative response.

And that was only the beginning of the marvelous communication method I had been given. The best was yet to come.

# NINE

The next several weeks were wonderful, for as the communicative training slowly gained momentum, every possible moment was filled with unfolding of the mysteries of God's creation. We learned of the Sons of God—consciousnesses that He created during an ancient research and development phase prior to His establishment of the physical system by which consciousness is currently created. We learned that the Sons of God, now highly evolved, serve Him as principal assistants in roles such as a Christ, a Holy Ghost, a Moses, a disciple, or a Buddha. They are also unique in that they were *serially* created, with each, in turn, having been initially formed from the actual substance of his predecessor. Were it to be graphed, therefore, their relationship to one another would appear much like the branches of a tree, or a system of roots.

He explained that I was of this lineage—and that I was not only a "Son of God," but *his* son, for I had been formed from him, long ago. Digressing somewhat, he explained that the term *Holy Ghost* describes the particular Son of God who administrates mankind during the period of a development cycle, or the time between Christs. The first Holy Ghost, he continued, was a Son of God who would be allegorically described, in the era subsequent to his administration, by the person of David, the biblical king of ancient Israel. But it was long, long before then, sometime in the eons that preceded even the formation of the earth, that an "offspring"[1] consciousness had been formed from this Son of God. And it was, he continued, in those dim recesses of time that of this offspring had he himself been formed. And then it was of him, in turn, that I had been formed.

He said that I, too, am a "root" of David.

Although the messages were now entirely mental, we continued for some time to use the white plastic pointer (we also found that a leaf or a business card worked just as well) for the purpose of verification. He would eventually wean me from its use entirely, however during this phase of the instruction it thankfully enabled the continued participation of my wife. The communicative training was a gradual process, therefore, but even at this early stage I found that, when alone, I was rapidly becoming proficient at carrying a practical conversation within my mind, during which verifications were accomplished by the strong, electric signal of affirmation—a signal which would one day have a very surprising added purpose.

There were many subtle variations to the instruction during this period, with the purposes thereof becoming evident only many months later. As an example, yet another process employed in the development of communicative

[1]Compare 1 Chronicles 17:11, also Revelation 22:16.

technique involved daily revisions to the New Testament, wherein the information surfaced within my mind not only as the familiar words and phrases but also as more complex mechanisms of perception. He required that I describe each revision in writing, then make corrections as necessary by asking questions of him and receiving either affirmations or additional information. I did not realize until later, of course, that these "revisions" were not really revisions at all, but *training*—for what lay ahead.

At that time I was also introduced to the concept of *pageant,* whereby individual consciousnesses are honed and refined through a process of affecting their apparent reality, or their seeming knowledge of what they see, hear, and understand. I was furthermore exposed to *intrusive emotion* as a device for educating the consciousness, and then provided with training and exercises whereby I learned to differentiate these processes from normal response characteristics within the psyche, or conscious intellect.

Eventually, this phase of the instruction drew to a close, an occasion that was to be marked by a marvelous gift: a vision.

# TEN

It was late one afternoon. We had been learning of the nature of creation—the physical process by which God creates and evolves consciousness. We had learned of the roles of the animal kingdoms, plants, and all forms of life up to and including mankind. And we had just asked about life on other worlds.

Needless to say, I was charmed when the thought of a "trip" suddenly surfaced in my mind. I said aloud, "Are you and I to take a trip of some sort?" and the electric currents within my back almost convulsed me with anticipation.

I closed my eyes, my wife by my side. For several minutes I saw nothing, then images like smoke rings appeared, flying forward, or—wait—I was flying *backward* through them! The apparent velocity increased as the images became more and more distinct; then, abruptly, they disappeared and were replaced by another image, tack-sharp and in incredible detail: a spiral galaxy. And it was approaching me (or I approaching it) at unbelievably high speed.

As I entered the galaxy, stars streamed by, each different and of incredible variety. Suddenly, a man's head loomed into view, totally obscuring perhaps one third of the total area of the vision. The head was in three-quarter profile, showing both the face and the right side of the head. It was a massive, strong, almost-animal face, with an extremely wide, straight chin and jaw, massive, angular facial features, and hair that was long, straight, stiff, and composed of extremely thick strands. The appearance was very much that of a lion-man,[1] complete with mane—with whom, in some subtle, inexplicable way, I felt a strange sense of identification.

The image remained for several minutes, fading as a second image formed: again, a man's head, however with a regal headdress and in frontal view. His handsome face was strong yet sensitive, with brown skin and almond eyes. The headdress was reminiscent of those worn by the pharaohs of ancient Egypt, however it rested on a thick golden band, or crown, that encircled his head. Extending prominently from the front of the crown, the massive golden head of a flying eagle balefully peered forward from just above his forehead.

The second image disappeared, and the stars hurtled by once more, only to be replaced moments later by atmosphere, and then by people—lovely people, happy people, but people with a difference: they were massive, had hair like manes, and looked very much like the first face in the vision. Suddenly they were gone, and I was hurtling backward through smoke ring images again.

Another galaxy then came into view, and the images of

[1]Compare Isaiah 52:14.

the lion-man and the eagle-man reappeared against the backdrop of moving stars. A familiar thought process briefly intruded upon my mind, advising me that the images were "calling cards" that identified us to the inhabitants of the world we were approaching. Realizing that one of the images was therefore associated with *me*, I instantly knew which it was. As the question formed in my mind, "Am I the lion-man?" my body convulsed with the electric pulses of verification. "Are you to be equated with the eagle-man?" was my next question—again, a strong verification.

Message received and understood: I was not only the Lamb, but the Lion too, and the Holy Ghost the Eagle.[2] What this new symbolism meant, however, I had yet to comprehend.

We then visited the second world on our itinerary, and I saw many of its people; by ones, twos, and threes, the exceedingly beautiful beings passed before my eyes. Incredibly, they appeared to be ordinary humans who had been—somehow—*improved*. In addition to their fine skin and striking physical beauty, each person seemed to be bathed in a soft, white light, and a peaceful, ethereal quality radiated from their countenances.

We withdrew from that world slowly, graciously; then, remaining within the same system, we visited its uninhabited worlds—in and out of colored atmospheres, clouds of strange hues and alien appearances, and all manner of wondrous sights.

The visits completed, we gradually departed the system, stopping briefly at something gigantic, awesome . . . *alien.* In fact, due to its proximity and immense size, I could

[2]Compare Revelation 4:7, 5:5.

initially see but a quarter of the huge, magnificent ship that hovered deep in space. Its construction was that of a central sphere from which thousands of giant rods projected radially outward; at the end of each rod, a system of three lesser rods cradled, much like the setting of a precious stone, a massive, pulsating, red jewel. As we departed, the distant appearance of the ship literally took my breath away—an immense, golden sphere, resplendent within its halo of pulsing, crimson lights.

Suddenly there were more smoke rings, more sensations of high speed, and then a third galaxy. Once again, my lion visage and his eagle visage appeared. Then a world of more people—people who looked cold—masses of people compressed tightly together, with thousands of faces in my field of view. An over-populated, oppressed, and stoic people.

The smoke rings abruptly reappeared, and then— nothing. Almost an hour had elapsed since the vision began, and now I was home.

# ELEVEN

I then began receiving information concerning "gifts" that had been bestowed upon me: To teach wisdom and knowledge; to prophesy; to judge; to receive and write the Word of God; and many, many others—the list encompassed all the ancient biblical gifts of the Holy Ghost known to man, except tongues and languages, and several very special new ones.

But now that my communicative skills had developed to the point of providing a useful dialogue, the underlying process by which these gifts operate was abundantly clear: they are each the result of communication. They are his actions, his will, his knowledge, his judgment—*communicated* to a mortal man.

As events progressed, I became increasingly aware of the communicative routine slowly maturing to one of relaxed but relatively continuous interaction, wherein I found myself guided on an almost constant basis in word and thought. I began to realize that I was becoming fully focused on what he needed to communicate, with no concern or desire on my part to do or say other than to reflect his bidding.

One morning, as I shaved, this developing relationship suddenly took on new definition as the following words were spoken into my mind in a clear, measured, and regal manner:

*All that thou understandeth is true, for I have given it unto you; for I am the Counselor and you the Spirit of Truth, who tells only what he hears.*[1]

Strong verifications underscored my correct comprehension of this latest wonder.

As I pondered this revelation during the day, an understanding of what was actually happening began to glimmer within my mind. And then the bombshell dropped.

[1]Compare John 16:12-15.

# TWELVE

It was late in December, only four months ago, and it came
by means of a dream. As with the dream several months
prior, after which the luminous balls hung over the bed,
this too was an experience of such remarkable realism and
clarity that I afterward remembered every single detail, as
I do to this day and probably always will.

I dreamed that I was walking into a giant compound,
having passed through a massive double gateway in a
massive wall that encircled the compound. The wall was
huge, monolithic, foreboding—and *expensive*, for although
it appeared to be of solid granite, it was nevertheless slightly
tapered, perfectly rounded at the top, and superbly finished, thereby giving the appearance of having been
erected at great monetary expense. It was not just an
ordinary granite wall, but a *fine* one.

Looking about the compound, I beheld a great monolithic structure at its center: a huge building that was
foreboding, massive, and again constructed of granite with
dark, matching windows. The granite blocks with which

the building was constructed were tapered, polished, and artfully blended; again, a structure that was not only dark, foreboding, powerful, and monolithic—but *expensive*.

I ascended the fine marble steps leading into the building. Looking into my hand, I found that it held a key of extraordinary mechanical complexity upon which hundreds of instructions were engraved in minute characters. I entered a nearby elevator, wishing to ascend thereby to a higher floor; unfortunately, however, I found that the elevator control panel not only required the key in my hand but that the panel itself was engraved with hundreds of additional instructions. As I studied the key and the control panel into which it was to be inserted, I slowly realized that they were both so unbelievably complex that it was not *possible* to understand how to make the elevator rise.

I gave up and began searching for stairs. In trying a nearby door, I came upon a giant room that was perhaps two stories high, seventy feet wide, and two hundred feet in length. The floor level of the room was located on the next lower level of the structure, therefore the doorway at which I stood was actually halfway up on one wall; a flight of stairs, with an intermediate platform and left-hand turn, led downward.

The room was full of expensive, high-technology equipment. At the far end of the room, banks of computers were attended by twenty to thirty men in long, black gowns. At the near end of the room, the wall was completely covered with hundreds of television screens, under which an expensive black marble counter was extravagantly laden with modern computer and video equipment. Operating the equipment were approximately twenty women who were uniformly clad in brief, skintight, futuristic garments of the same black fabric as worn by the men.

My gaze shifted to the television screens, which displayed various portions of a gigantic mob of ordinary, common people. The mob was moving, it was miserable, and the cameras to which the television screens connected were focused upon its misery.

One of the television screens showed a member of the mob falling, and then being trampled. Many were focused on a portion of the mob that had raised a young woman above their heads; she was helpless, crying, and tormented, and the television screens impassively observed her plight.

The remaining screens focused on other aspects of the mob, but always upon its misery. And as I stood transfixed by what I saw, I suddenly realized that the television screens were monitors, and that the images thereon were being produced for the pleasure of others in the giant structure.

I raced out of the building to keep from throwing up.

I ran down the outside steps, across the compound, and out the huge gateway. I stopped outside, having noticed as I ran that a fragile and ineffectual wooden wall surrounded the massive granite barrier, perhaps twenty feet beyond. An outer enclosure was thereby created, within which were hundreds of men wearing long, black gowns. Sharply defined against the black fabric, a single ornament hung prominently from a chain about each man's neck.

In the distance I could see the mob approaching.

One of the men ran to me with a container. "Cup your hands," he said urgently, proceeding then to fill my hands with water. "This is all we have to protect ourselves!" he cried over his shoulder as he ran for the protection of the flimsy outer wall.

Horrified, I spun around, dropped the useless water on the ground, and ran back inside the compound. As I ran, I heard a giant bell utter a single, massive, reverberating note, the sound of which was "ommmmm"—it was a death knell. I stopped, turned around, and saw the gates closing behind me. As they closed completely, they were securely locked and bolted by a person wearing a long, scarlet robe and a tall headdress; the robe and headdress were very elegant and stately, having been richly embellished with fine cloths and embroidery.

I ran back up the fine marble steps which were now covered with loathsome reptilian creatures of perhaps six to eighteen inches in length. They appeared to be of a variety of shapes, however their common characteristics were that they were abominable, repulsive, disgusting— and everywhere. I ran inside the building, down the hall, and to the door of the room that contained the video monitors. Flinging open the door, I ran down the stairs to the floor level, barely avoiding the reptilian abominations that now covered the stairs. Suddenly I stopped and looked about me, for something was different: the people were gone . . . no, they were not gone, but *changed*. The people who had been in the room *were* the loathsome reptilian abominations, and they were everywhere.

I ran up the stairs, through the hallway, and down the outside steps. And as I ran, I realized something peculiar: I knew deep within that some of the abominations were not real, but only *pageant*.[1] Somehow I could detect these

[1]*Pageant:* defined in Chapter 9.

as I ran and thereby place my feet only on the ones I knew were not real; my feet would pass through them to solid footing underneath, enabling me to safely sprint from the building.

And then I awoke.

It was 4 a.m. and still dark outside. I went downstairs to the living room, my mind alive with detailed recollection of the dream. I sat down on the couch and looked about for something with which to occupy my time. I picked up the Bible, began idly flipping the pages, then stopped as something in the tenth chapter of Isaiah caught my interest—something about ancient Assyria. As I read the first several verses of the chapter, a strange, intense feeling of tension and familiarity began to form within my mind. I read the verses again, and then cried out, "Oh my God, it's the Catholic Church!" as the dream and the verses collided into solid understanding, and heavy waves of verification, now *centrally* located within my body, swept up and down, up and down, up and down from scalp to heels until I was almost exhausted.

## THIRTEEN

New information and sensations were now assailing me at a tremendous rate; yet, for some reason that I could not comprehend, I was easily adapting to the flood of input without becoming overloaded mentally or emotionally.

As I considered the events of the last few minutes, I was drawn more to the unusual verification that I had experienced only moments before. Whereas the Holy Ghost always caused a strong, electric, pulsating sensation in the upper right-hand side of my back as a signal of affirmation, this latest occurrence was similar except that it was *centrally* located, ran the length of my body, and was many orders of magnitude stronger. It was with a certain trepidation, therefore, that I asked within my mind, "Holy Ghost—was that verification from you?"

No response.

"Was it *not* from you?"

I felt the usual affirmative response in the upper right-hand side of my back.

Who was it from? The question kept circling in my mind, followed always by the same answer I was almost afraid to voice. I summoned the courage and said, this time aloud, "Dear God—was that you?"

Strong, centrally located waves of affirmation washed up and down, up and down my body in response.

Then, abruptly, the familiar mental communications began again. But now they were intense, purposed, complex, and efficient, as the strong sensations within my nervous system simultaneously provided a running commentary of verification. The combined communicative paths began to feel, quite simply, like talking to someone who was within me—sharing my skin, as it were—but someone warm, loving, and immeasurably intelligent. And then I suddenly realized what Jesus meant when he said that the Father was *in* him:[1] He was in intimate communicative contact that he could *feel within his body,* in the same manner as I was now experiencing. More waves of verification underscored this remarkable understanding.

As this marvelous communication took hold, my understandings advanced by quantum leaps, and always through a similar process: As with a student sitting at the feet of his teacher, I would hear, within my mind, a perfectly articulated commentary or discourse, occasionally punctuated by extraordinary, nonverbal gestalts of meaning. I would mentally explore the information, ask questions and receive answers, receive additional commentary—and then, as understanding dawned, the strong waves of verification would signal my correct comprehension. Conceptually complex information, I would discover in the days and weeks to come, would generally be preceded by a dream such as the one I had just experienced, or perhaps a daytime

[1]John 14:10.

vision, thereby creating an efficient perceptual framework upon which the subsequent mental communications would build.

That morning, as I pondered these miraculous gifts of knowledge and understanding, I was suddenly drawn back to the dream of only an hour or so before which had started it all. The instruction now began in earnest as I found myself directed to read various passages, interspersed with appropriate mental discourse, from the Bible and latter-day revelation.

My understanding developed rapidly: The Catholic Church—the centuries-old genesis of a system of doctrinal theology that has efficiently corrupted and perverted something so magnificent, so wonderful, and now so completely alien to human understanding that the Church and its theological progeny have become the very antithesis of that which they purportedly represent.

In having tacitly removed from a major segment of mankind's collective memory the revealed knowledge of reincarnation, of the continual cycles of man's development, and of the respective Lambs of these cycles, the Church is the express fulfillment of not only the "abomination that makes desolate" of Daniel,[2] but also of the "great church, mother of abominations" of the Book of Mormon.[3] Even more significant to our understanding, however, it is also . . . *Assyria!*

---

[2]Daniel 11:31, 12:11. Compare Matthew 24:15, concerning the sign of Daniel.
[3]Compare 1 Nephi 13:26-28, the Book of Mormon.

## FOURTEEN

*From this time forth I make you hear new things, hidden things which you have not known. . . . before today you have never heard of them, lest you should say, "Behold, I knew them." You have never heard, you have never known, from of old your ear has not been opened.* (Isaiah 48:6-8)

The Bible is not about history; the Bible is about consciousness, reincarnation, and the system God has implemented to form, develop, grow, and refine consciousness. That which we perceive as the inner self—our private, internal, individual self—is the sole purpose for the existence of the *entire physical system,* including worlds, plants, animals, our bodies, insects, galaxies, and natural laws. It is all a vast educational mechanism—a *school*—created and maintained for the development of consciousness from nursery to maturity. Mankind is the highest level of this reincarnational system, following which a fully developed consciousness (or "soul") takes his place in the natural environment which the Bible refers to as Heaven.

Many thousands of years are required for one's consciousness to develop through the grades and levels of mankind, with each step of the way guided by the Sons of

56

God. Working under the direction of the Holy Ghost, the Sons of God are assisted in their work by past "graduates" of the system.

Conceptually similar to the highest grade in an earthly school, the group which we shall refer to as the "graduating class" represents the highest level of the school of mankind—a level that has currently required two thousand years to complete.

Two thousand years ago, the prior class graduated. Their Lamb was an individual now known only as John the Baptist; working under the direction of the then-current Holy Ghost, he physically initiated the earthly events that subtly, almost imperceptibly, culminated in the passing of a graduating class from mankind into the natural realm we know of as Heaven.

As these events unfolded, the Holy Ghost came as Jesus the Christ to initiate the complex path over which mankind would be led during the period of the current graduating class, which was then forming. The beginning of a new phase in the mass lesson plan for man, the path he established was lovingly and intentionally designed to force us to grow and to make us efficiently develop into the mature, loving, caring, advanced conscious beings we are all capable of becoming.

Much as a child is sent to school with the requirement that he perform his schoolwork well regardless of his understanding of the purpose of the lessons, so mankind is similarly provided with lessons, tests, more lessons and more tests. It is a system designed by God and lovingly administered by the Holy Ghost and his staff of highly evolved assistants. It is a system of mercy and caring; a system of individual attention to those who strive to know and perform His will; and a system of justice for those who flagrantly ignore His will. Those students who graduate are glorified. Those students who consistently ignore their teachers are expelled—*extinguished.*

And now, of the graduating class that formed two thousand years ago, those who have learned their lessons well are graduating to everlasting glory. When it's all over, a new graduating class will be formed from mankind, and the coming Christ will initiate a new path over which mankind will travel in its studies.

That is what the Bible is about. And this is how it works:

# FIFTEEN

The society of man is characterized by a number of seemingly unshakable institutions and establishments, such as medicine, law, science, government, bureaucracy, natural resource monopoly, finance, and a host of organized religions. Rather than the result of some random process, however, the appearance of these institutions in society is far from accidental; they are *stress-test crucibles* established by God to forge, purify, refine, develop, and test the advanced consciousness of man.

Each time a person's consciousness reincarnates (a continual process until one either graduates or is extinguished), it receives two fundamental gifts for its new journey through life: The first is a physical body, in which physical senses very much like the natural senses of one's consciousness provide sensory input through an interface or connective organ known as the brain. Thinking, learning, feeling, seeing, hearing, remembering, identity—all are natural characteristics of the consciousness, with the brain and body simply enabling one to operate within the physical environment of the "school" conducted by God. Of all the natural characteristics of the consciousness, only past memories are left unconnected to the new physical body, so that the decisions and responses of life will be true reflections of one's maturing personality.[1]

Each person's consciousness is thereby connected to physical reality by his external senses. But there is also a second connection provided—one that is every bit as real and infinitely more important: *Every consciousness existing in physical reality is connected to God's will,* a connection that is manifested in mankind by conscience, or an internal "knowing" of right from wrong. And it is upon this holy connection—this internal perception of right and wrong—that His entire system turns.

Our world and our society are intentionally designed to not only nurture us, but to also test, refine, and stress us, and cause us to grow. We are given commandments; we are given the perception of right and wrong; and we are given sophisticated stress-test crucibles to tempt us away from what we know is right, deep down inside.

The most severe stress-test crucible of modern times, for example, has formed about the Catholic Church, in which one is coerced to worship graven images and idols; in which innumerable dead persons ("saints") are placed between oneself and God through proclamation of men in fine robes; and in which massive amounts of rules, regulations, and doctrine subtly confuse and pervert one's internal connection with God. The soul who has successfully passed this test is not the one who listens to the Catholic Church

---

[1]Compare Matthew 12:43-44.

and follows its direction through either fear or acceptance. The soul who has successfully passed this test has left the Catholic Church—because it did not feel right, deep down inside.

## SIXTEEN

The Bible, as a textbook for the school of mankind, must simultaneously encompass the needs of consciousnesses at many levels of development. It is therefore largely written at two levels of meaning, and sometimes more, using a sophisticated form of allegory in which the literal meaning is intended to educate, and the underlying (or allegorical) meaning is intended to reward—at the end of the age—with the Truth.

As with teaching a child in terms it can comprehend by using lessons and examples to which it can relate, the literal meanings of the Bible provide the developing consciousness with important moral and spiritual values; with commandments and laws to reinforce the perception of right and wrong; with examples of God-seeking behavior to emulate; with intentionally confusing promises and hopes that will cause one to struggle to understand and thereby achieve more. And the literal meanings all *seem* to describe actual physical things and events, so that they can be comprehended and accepted by a still-immature consciousness—by one who is still growing.

But the Bible holds a marvelous message in the under-lying meaning of its educational allegories—a very special message for those whose perception and understanding have grown to the highest level in mankind and who are about to graduate:

The words of Jesus, the words of God, the covenants, the prophecies, and the majority of the events of religious history in the entire Bible from Genesis to Revelation are about *consciousness.* They are about the nurturing and development of consciousness; they are about the great stress-test crucibles established by God to forge and refine consciousness; they are about the prior graduations from mankind; and they are about this graduation.

And it is all written in a unique form of allegory that is absolutely consistent from cover to cover; a form of allegory that could not be known until it was given of God, thereby providing a simple and effective means of security for the message and the sign:

He planned it thousands of years ago; furthermore, He wrote it all down to prove it to us!

# SEVENTEEN

*An evil and adulterous generation seeks for a sign; but no
sign shall be given to it except the sign of the prophet Jonah.*
(Matthew 12:39)

Having generally treated the subjects necessary to provide
context, the instruction then progressively concentrated
upon the detailed allegories of the Bible. It was a fairly
lengthy undertaking, for the basis of biblical allegory rests
in the processes of the surrounding larger reality within
which the physical universe has its existence, requiring
therefore that one achieve a rudimentary knowledge of
this greater reality prior to understanding the allegory. As
though by design, however, there are many fine gradations
to the allegory, enabling it to be used as a highly functional
teaching tool wherein each step understood enhances one's
preparation for the next step to be undertaken.

Consistent with its purpose, the allegory also embraces
a comprehensive hierarchy of words with double meaning,
including many common words of which one would not
ordinarily suspect dual meaning—such as the noun *generation,* which allegorically refers to the period of a graduating
class, or the time between Christs. There is, however, one

major subset of these biblical "codewords" that is reasonably straightforward and thereby fairly easy to comprehend: Geographical place-names and names of tribes, kingdoms, or other groups of people actually refer to specific stress-test crucibles, specific groups of consciousnesses, or the physical persons in whom a specific group of consciousnesses are incarnate.

*Assyria,* for example, refers to the Catholic Church stress-test crucible. Nineveh (ancient capital of Assyria) therefore represents the Vatican hierarchy, and the king of Assyria (or the king of Nineveh) represents the Pope. An example of these allegorical terms in use may be found in the book of Jonah, in which God proclaims Nineveh's wickedness and promises to overthrow it in forty days. And in which the king of Nineveh repents and instructs his subjects to also repent and turn from their evil ways, in the hope that He might yet show them mercy. The book of Jonah is not a simple story of a whale; it is a clear, pointed message to the Catholic hierarchy that was prepared over two thousand years ago, before the very inception of that Church. And its time is *now.*[1]

Other names and their meanings include *Israel,* which refers collectively to all consciousnesses incarnate in mankind; also *Judah,* which refers to physical mankind. Additional names used in the biblical allegory-code include *Jacob, Levi, Edom, Ammon, Moab, Ephraim, Tyre, Sidon, Chaldea, Babylon, Egypt, Kittim, Joseph,* and scores of others. Furthermore, these allegorical terms are also to be found within the Book of Mormon, the Koran, and the Dead Sea Scrolls,

---

[1]Compare Matthew 12:39-41, 16:2-4.

abundantly and correctly utilized within the specific context of a common allegorical structure that is only now being revealed—an allegorical structure that has never before been known to man.

Within this revelation, therefore, inherently lies the clear understanding of the covenants, the prophecies, and the whole of scriptural antiquity.

He has thus far spent over two months with me on this one subject alone. The information received is vast and unimaginably rich, touching not only the known sacred writings of our world but many not yet realized to have originated Above. The sheer overwhelming magnitude of the information, however, renders its written exposition fundamentally inconsistent with the purpose he has set for this book. But he says there will soon be a second *Book of the Lamb,* and there the exposition will begin.

## EIGHTEEN

As the instruction continued, I found myself continually reflecting upon the extraordinary speed with which I was learning not only facts but massive new concepts involving the very nature of our reality; at some level, it seemed almost as though I had once known the material and was merely being allowed to remember it. Each day my curiosity grew until it reached almost the point of bursting, however in my role of student I did not feel I should press for an answer; he would tell me in his own good time, I hoped.

Thus it was with a sense of impending relief that one day I found myself compulsively praying aloud, for the third time in this most amazing process, the words that had suddenly overwhelmed my mind: "Dear God—I learn these concepts so fast. Is there more to *me* than I understand?"

That evening the answer came in a brief perceptual revelation of only a few moments duration. The words suddenly sprang into my mind, "You are more than you realize; ask for a sample of your natural self!" So I did—and the next few moments were filled with the most incredible experience yet: high-speed thought communication. I virtually reeled under the unexpected onslaught of fully formed, discrete thought gestalts that poured into my mind at a rate of at least ten per second. Each was a comprehensive, instantaneous, wordless packet of information. To use an analogy, they were not words or sentences but larger organizations of information that were more like chapters; furthermore, many incorporated elaborate visual images and other sensory data—*whatever was necessary* to make the information module complete. Even more astounding, my mind easily and comfortably perceived and retained the content of each.

A few moments later, it was gone. But now I *knew*.

I had previously been informed that I was a highly evolved Son of God—one of many—but what that meant personally had never really penetrated, for I had never *felt* highly evolved. It was now apparent, however, that those perceptions had been carefully, lovingly, but thoroughly blocked; that I had been intellectually confounded all my life; that I had been intentionally provided a constant stream of emotions and thoughts to confuse me, stress me, control my actions and perceptions, and camouflage me from both myself and others. Until now. I was becoming *un*confounded, and I knew it.

That night came the dream. As with the others, this dream was an experience of such realism and uncompromising visual quality that I could afterward recall each and every detail, as I can to this day. It was a very special dream with a very special message. A very *precious* message.

It began with a boy—a bright, smiling, calm, self-assured

boy of perhaps twelve years of age; a fresh haircut and clean, pressed clothes lent him a well-scrubbed, wholesome appearance. As I walked past him I noticed that he was holding a second clean, freshly pressed suit of clothes in front of him, as though he expected someone to arrive soon who needed them. He smiled warmly as I walked by.

I was tall, mature, white-haired, and wore a full-length white gown. Clutching my right hand was a small child of perhaps three whom I knew was in my care; he was a happy, vivacious, intelligent, and thoroughly charming child who babbled gaily as we walked. We entered a restroom, whereupon I lovingly lifted him onto the seat of a white commode. His childish tumble of words continued unabated as he centered himself, suspended in mid-air, on the adult-sized white ring.

He talked happily and incessantly, as would any bright and well-adjusted child, not noticing that as he talked the white ring was growing larger and the commode deeper— much deeper—until it became a cesspool. Suddenly he fell in, disappearing beneath the surface of the filth below.

A few moments later he surfaced, no longer babbling gaily but now fighting for his life. Although he was covered with filth, his teeth were clenched resolutely, and his bright eyes were frightened yet strangely self-assured as they gazed up at me. I knew that he knew I would help him, but that it was his responsibility to meet me halfway.

Hanging by my feet from the outer edge, I eased myself into the cesspool cavity, headfirst, with my hand outstretched to him as he bravely confronted his reality in the filth below. He reached up for my hand, but in vain—it was too far. I managed to lower myself another few inches while he bravely and quietly fought even harder, managing

69

to reach even higher on his second attempt; but still he fell back. He tried again and again, each time more bravely and more resolutely than before, and each time realizing that the higher he reached, the further down I could reach.

Suddenly, our hands met in a firm, mutual grip. I lovingly pulled him from the cesspool; then, I gently bathed him so that he would be spotlessly clean. He smiled confidently as he was brought the clean, freshly pressed suit of clothes—and I noticed that he looked older now.

I awoke; and I knew, deep inside, what it means to be a Son of God. I realized that those who are in the process of maturing through mankind are *all* children in the sight of God. I realized that the most significant difference between a Son of God and a child of God is one of time, for the Sons of God are much older and more mature, and therefore bear major responsibilities with regard to the nurturing and care of His children.

As feelings of sadness engulfed me, I also realized what it means to undergo travail for the sins of others: It is an incredibly loving act for a mature consciousness—one who has been beyond the physical system for eons—to incarnate. To leave a realm of loving, gracious, kind and nurturing companions, and of close association with God. And to willingly subject oneself to temporary memory erasure, a cumbersome body that feels pain, and a system designed to forge, refine, and hone the still-immature developing consciousnesses of mankind through a lovingly applied but very real program of stress, confusion, suffering, and exposure to evil.

To return to physical existence for the purpose of helping His children is an act of service to the Creator of the highest order; and there are thousands who have done it for this graduation and who are on earth at this very moment.

The Resurrection has been quietly in progress for many years.

# NINETEEN

*Believe therefore in God and his apostles, and say not,
"Three:" (there is a Trinity)—Forbear—it will be better for
you. God is only one God!* (Sura 4:171, the Koran)

As I learned more of the system He has created for the
development and maturing of consciousness, I began to
perceive something that I had not expected. Eventually the
perception mushroomed into yet another fully formed
compulsion, whereupon I asked, "Does our consciousness
continue to develop and grow *after* it is mature?" Strong
verifications signalled a correct understanding. "Do the
Sons of God continue to evolve?" Again, the affirmation.
"Does the entire system of consciousnesses, including current graduates, past graduates, Sons of God—and even
God himself—continually evolve?" A strong, centrally
located verification underscored this remarkable understanding and opened the way to a revelation of staggering
proportions—and staggering simplicity. Because, after all,
the Christs evolve too.

The Sons of God are ancient consciousnesses—proto-
types handmade by God before the physical system

was placed in operation. The process required vast eons of time, and involved the fabrication of a first perfected consciousness. Then, much as an orchard-keeper finding himself possessed of a perfect tree would remove a sprig and nurture it separately to obtain a second perfect tree, so were the subsequent Sons of God created one from the other. A portion of the first perfected consciousness was nurtured, developed, and became the second perfected consciousness; a portion of the second perfected consciousness was nurtured, developed, and became the third perfected consciousness; and so on, creating a chain of "firstborn" perfected consciousnesses to bear the ultimate responsibility: the management of the developing consciousnesses of earth.

The reigning Son of God is known as the Holy Ghost; he is "in charge" of God's system for the maturing of consciousness for a complete development cycle, or the period between Christs. Assisting the Holy Ghost is his firstborn, who is known as the Lamb. And with each cycle—each graduation from mankind—each coming of a Christ—the mantle is passed, Father to Son.

As each development cycle concludes, many Sons of God incarnate in key positions to insure the correct implementation of events. The Lamb incarnates to gather the graduates and prepare for the Christ. The Holy Ghost provides the gift of awareness to the graduates, then comes as Christ to complete the development cycle and set the stage for the next cycle and the new graduating class.

The cycle of a generation having been thus completed, all have evolved. The graduates have evolved to mature consciousnesses in the natural environment we know of as Heaven. The Christ has evolved to more than a Christ.

73

The Lamb has evolved to Holy Ghost. The firstborn of the Lamb has evolved to Lamb. The lesser Sons of God have evolved. The consciousnesses of mankind who do God's will have evolved and are closer to their own graduation day. And during this period, the mature consciousnesses already in Heaven—the *past* graduates—have evolved, according to their service to God.

And even God has evolved.

Long ago, during the period of the very first graduating class from mankind, the Holy Ghost was a firstborn Son of God by the name of *Yhwh*[1]—the "David" of biblical allegory. Assisting him was his understudy—his Lamb—his firstborn, a Son of God who would be known thousands of years later as Jesus. When the first class was ready to graduate, *Yhwh* came as the first Christ and Messiah, his Lamb preceding him to gather the graduates and make ready for his coming. The graduates were given the gift of knowledge of their destiny, and then events were set in motion that would further refine, nurture, and develop mankind during the period of the second graduating class, which was then forming.

When it was all over, and the earthly lives of the participants had ended, the graduates found themselves to be fully mature consciousnesses in the natural environment we know of as Heaven. *Yhwh* had gone to beyond-a-Christ, performing service to his creator—and ours—at an incomprehensibly high level. The mantle of Holy Ghost for the

---

[1]*Yhwh* is a transliteration of the "Divine Name," as written in consonantal ancient Hebrew. I have used this form because neither *Yahweh* nor *Jehovah*, both of which are modern doctrinal reconstructions, reasonably reflect the pronunciation used by the Holy Ghost in his communications.

period of the second graduating class then fell on his Lamb, who would come millennia later as the second Christ and Messiah, Jesus. And the Lamb of Jesus was *his* firstborn, a Son of God who would be known as the prophet Jeremiah, as Buddha, as John the Baptist, and as a disciple of Jesus (John the Baptist was also one of the twelve disciples; several seemingly individual characters portray this one person in the Bible to aid in concealing the true nature of the event).

Once again the cycle of the ages was reborn, for after the second graduating class had gone to glory; after Jesus had come as Christ; after his Lamb had incarnated as John the Baptist (also a disciple) to gather the graduates; after the participants' earthly lives had ended—after it was all over, a third graduating class had been convened, and all of mankind who do God's will had evolved. Jesus had evolved to beyond-a-Christ, proceeding onward to serve God, his creator as well as ours, at more advanced levels. The mantle of Holy Ghost then fell on Jesus' Lamb, his firstborn, who had last incarnated as John the Baptist (also a disciple). And whose Lamb in turn is *his* firstborn, a Son of God who has incarnated as the prophet Mohammed and as the prophet Joseph Smith. Unbelievable as it may seem, I am apparently he—Lamb of the Holy Ghost and of the coming Christ and Messiah. Lamb of he who is so much more than I that I am not fit to scrape his shoes. Lamb of the Lord of the Earth.

And this time, the graduates will come from the entire world.

Although the Sons of God are relatively few in number, over the centuries a particular Son of God may appear to be many different individuals as he incarnates to serve in various roles. This is especially true of the Lambs, who incarnate specifically to receive God's Word as dictated by the Holy Ghost, for in this manner did all authentic holy scriptures come into existence. In this manner was the enlightenment of Buddha received, the original scriptures of the New Testament received by John the Baptist (also a disciple), the Koran received by the prophet Mohammed, the Book of Mormon received by the prophet Joseph Smith, and most of the books of the Old Testament received by the Lambs before me.

There is yet another role for the Lamb, for as in the story of Jonah, the biblical tale of Elijah also carries an important message in its allegorical meaning: It describes the final incarnation of a Lamb, wherein he prepares the graduates and makes ready for the end of the development cycle. It has described the final incarnation of two Lambs before me, and now it apparently describes mine. It seems that I am also Elijah, who is to restore all things—with the Truth.

When the Holy Ghost appears to his incarnate Lamb during a development cycle, he may also assume various identities such that the resulting written record is consistent with the state of development and awareness of the consciousnesses for whom it is intended. For example, our present Holy Ghost—the coming Christ—was the angel Gabriel who gave the Koran to Mohammed; he was the angel Moroni who gave the Book of Mormon to Joseph Smith; and he is himself as he gives us the Books of the Lamb.

All the disciples of Jesus were incarnate Sons of God, as will be the disciples of the coming Christ, most of whom are already incarnate. These, plus additional Sons of God,

76

have been incarnating as both men and women for years, and as they mature physically have been maneuvered into key roles within our society, worldwide. Most of the incarnate Sons of God are still confounded, so that their purpose, their identity, and their abilities are totally hidden—even from themselves.

In addition to the few Sons of God, thousands of past graduates have also quietly incarnated, have also been maneuvered into key roles within our society, and are also confounded. The Sons of God are in important, primary roles that involve the origination and implementation of action, whereas the past graduates are in lesser roles wherein they will assure the correct flow of information and events. Incarnate, mature, but confounded consciousnesses now permeate mankind—in position—needing only to be unconfounded as required. The society of man has been *infiltrated,* and the unfolding of God's plan for these times is under direct and complete control.

In the course of my own unconfounding, I have been given knowledge of the identity of many other incarnate Sons of God and the key roles to which they are assigned, however I am directed by the Holy Ghost to record the name of but one in this book. And never before, since the earth began, has a Son of God incarnated in the role of he whose name I am to record. He has been placed in this role solely because he will know God's will—he will know what to do. He is Pope John Paul II of the Roman Catholic Church.

# TWENTY

The final book of the Bible was then opened wide, as he painstakingly explained the meaning of the Revelation to John.

It began with the seven seals, which were opened one by one as the full meaning of the planned catastrophes and the resultant shockwaves for humanity was described and revealed, as was the mechanism by which these events shall occur.

The meaning of the fall of Babylon was described, as were the beasts of the Revelation. The manner by which Satan will be dethroned—indeed, the mechanism of sin and evil itself was revealed. The new Jerusalem, the Resurrection, Judgment—all were revealed. Everything. And all of it functionally identical to the prophecies of the Old Testament, the Book of Mormon, and the Koran.

As with the biblical allegory, however, I am told that the complete written exposition of this information is to begin in *The Second Book of the Lamb*. But the following are to be revealed now:

*He who has an ear, let him hear what the Spirit says to the churches. To him who conquers I will grant to eat of the tree of life, which is in the paradise of God.*
(Revelation 2:7)

*He who conquers shall be clad thus in white garments, and I will not blot his name out of the book of life; I will confess his name before my Father and before his angels.*
(Revelation 3:5)

It begins with the new graduate—"he who conquers"[1]—one who has taken all the courses in mankind, passed all the tests, and is quietly being fitted for cap and gown. One who will no longer reincarnate. One who has grown in grace and awareness through centuries of following God's will until his consciousness has become fully mature. One who will soon find himself in the natural environment we know of as Heaven. One who is becoming eternal. A mature child of God, in whom He is well pleased.

*Weep not; lo, the Lion of the tribe of Judah, the Root of David, has conquered, so that he can open the scroll and its seven seals. And between the throne and the four living creatures and among the elders, I saw a Lamb standing, as though it had been slain . . . .*
(Revelation 5:5-6)

I have opened the seals. I am the Lion (from the vision) of the tribe of Judah (allegorical codeword for physical mankind). I am a Root of David (a firstborn descendant

---

[1]"He who overcometh" in King James.

79

of the Son of God allegorically described as David), and I conquered long ago.[2]

And on June 27, 1844, the prophet Joseph Smith was brutally assassinated by an armed mob at Carthage jail, in Carthage, Illinois. Thus was the Lamb slain, in fulfillment of prophecy.

*They came to life, and reigned with Christ a thousand years. The rest of the dead did not come to life until the thousand years were ended. This is the first resurrection. Blessed and holy is he who shares in the first resurrection!*
(Revelation 20:4-6)

Within this prophecy, *the dead* is an allegorical term used to describe one's post-death self in a way that intentionally conceals the mechanism of reincarnation. To those existing in centuries past, for whom this prophecy was written, we *are* the dead.

The term *resurrection* is descriptive of the graduation process, which ultimately involves one's passage from physical existence to the natural realm of consciousness and its context of immortal life. In such a manner do the "dead" come to "life."

The initial phase of the graduation process is the temporary return to earth, by means of incarnation and physical birth, of the Sons of God and past graduates who are to actually implement the graduation. At the conclusion of the process, *all* return to the natural realm—Sons of God,

---

[2]I must emphasize that I do not make these claims, but rather reiterate the information he has given me—*he* makes these claims. Qualified persons may verify this information for themselves using the method to be presented in the next chapter.

past graduates, and new graduates alike—through a gradual metamorphosis (or "transfiguration") wherein they are methodically and consciously divested of the restraints of physical reality.

And for those who are not yet ready to graduate, the next class—"the rest of the dead"—will graduate in a thousand years.[3]

> *And I saw the dead, great and small, standing before the throne, and books were opened. Also another book was opened, which is the book of life. And the dead were judged by what was written in the books, by what they had done.*
> (Revelation 20:12)

Judgment Day—a specter for centuries, yet now with a very straightforward meaning: it is discovering your destiny. It is finding out whether you are graduating or you are not. If you are not graduating, you are probably still within the process of development and will continue to grow in grace and awareness as you prepare to graduate with a future class. If you are not graduating and you flagrantly and constantly disregard God's will, your consciousness may be in danger of being extinguished after this life.

There has been a way provided for you to find out if you are graduating, and if you are, to help you learn what you are to do: it is the promise of the white stone. For if you are graduating—going to Heaven—you will "receive" one.

Also among those who receive the white stone will be

---

[3]Compare 1 Nephi 12:11-12, the Book of Mormon.

the confounded ones—the incarnate past graduates and Sons of God. They may be led to yet another step of discovery, or "judgment," and this is how it works:

*When the Spirit of Truth comes, he will guide you into all the truth; for he will not speak on his own authority, but whatever he hears he will speak . . . .*
(John 16:13)

*He shall not judge by what his eyes see, or decide by what his ears hear; but with righteousness he shall judge . . . .*
(Isaiah 11:3-4)

As the Lamb, I have been taught to clearly receive and verify communication from the Holy Ghost. All that I "hear" is from within my mind and body, therefore ears play no part in my communication with him. All that I have told you has been learned in this way, and all that I will tell you in the future shall come in this way. Furthermore, if you have received the white stone and are led to ask, he has instructed me to tell you what you are: whether new graduate, past graduate, or Son of God.

For each person who has received the white stone and who asks of me to do so, I shall inquire thus of the Holy Ghost—no more, no less. And I will tell you the answer I receive.

Blessed and holy are the men, women, and children who receive the white stone, for they are those who are invited to the marriage supper of the Lamb.[4]

---

[4]Revelation 19:9.

# TWENTY-ONE

*But the stone that struck the image became a great mountain and filled the whole earth.* (Daniel 2:35)

The white stone—a gift from Heaven that is only for the redeemed of the earth. It is knowledge, it is communication, it is verification of your decree of judgment, and it is the beginning of your transfiguration.

It has been used many times before, by prophets, by Lambs, and by each generation to be harvested from the earth. Beginning therefore with the first Lamb and the first graduating class, one may find it recorded in the story of the exodus, which, as with the story of Jonah, allegorically describes something quite different from its apparent literal meaning. It tells of the first Israelites (allegorical codeword for the consciousnesses of mankind) being redeemed from the first major stress-test crucible (codeword *Egypt*). It tells of Aaron's "breastpiece of judgment,"[1] upon which were the Urim and Thummim that were used to inquire of the LORD.[2] It tells of how the Israelites

---

[1]Exodus 28:30.
[2]Translators have replaced the name *Yhwh* with the capitalized word *LORD* (source: Preface to the Revised Standard Version, Second Edition).

received manna (allegorical codeword for knowledge and understanding of heavenly things)—just as you will, if you are graduating. And how it all started with their white stones:

> *In the evening quails came up and covered the camp; and in the morning the dew lay round about the camp. And when the dew had gone up, there was on the face of the wilderness a fine, flake-like thing . . . .* (Exodus 16:13-14)

Moses and Aaron used it; Joseph Smith used it; John the Baptist and Jesus used it; two past graduating classes have used it, and I've used it. And if you "receive" one, you must use it. Although it differs slightly from age to age in its physical implementation, its function is always the same. Whether it is known as an Urim, a Thummim, a fine flake-like thing, or a white stone—whether it is larger or smaller or fancy or plain—it makes no difference, for the thing itself has no properties that influence its behavior.

It is simply a small piece of matter; a tiny thing that can be easily moved about, by persons or by angels. It is used by two persons at once, each resting a finger or two upon it so that only they are aware of the source of its movement. To the observer, it appears that the stone is moved by the two persons. But the two persons, however, are aware that the stone moves independently; that they are actually *following* the stone as it is moved by a mature consciousness from Heaven:

> *So it will be at the close of the age. The angels will come out and separate the evil from the righteous . . . .*
> (Matthew 13:49)

If you are of the redeemed, or perhaps a past graduate,

the Holy Ghost will one day soon provide a Teacher—a mature consciousness in Heaven—an *angel*—to speak with you, for it is actual communication from such a being that constitutes "receiving" a white stone. If you receive such communication, you are of the redeemed. If you do not receive such communication, you are not. It is just that simple.

The day and hour at which your initial communication will occur and also the degree or length of such communication will vary greatly, depending upon the individual role you are to fulfill as one of the redeemed. You are to diligently pursue such communication, however, until the day comes that you *do* receive your white stone:

> *To him who conquers I will give some of the hidden manna, and I will give him a white stone, with a new name written on the stone which no one knows except him who receives it.* (Revelation 2:17)[3]

When the day arrives that an angel communicates with you in this manner, he will give you a name by which you may identify him. It will be a simple name, most probably consisting of only a few letters—perhaps as few as one or two—but it will be a name that is fully adequate to define the individual with whom you are communicating. Owing to their brevity, such names may appear to be strange and may even be a sequence of letters that cannot be pronounced but must be spelled; nonetheless, this is the manner in which advanced consciousnesses have identified themselves to mortals since the system began.

Before attempting to communicate, place a Bible nearby

---

[3]Compare *Doctrine and Covenants* 130:9-11 (reproduced on p. 103).

for reference. Stop and reflect for a few moments. Remember that, if successful, you will be communicating with a being in Heaven who is considerably more advanced and mature than you. One who is accustomed to the kindness, consideration, grace, and loving ways of mature consciousness. One who is superior to you in all ways. One who is there to teach you.

Therefore, be reverent, be kind, be considerate, and be loving as you offer to speak with your Teacher. And be patient, always remembering that it is the teacher who knows what the student needs—not the student. In other words, if any instructions you may receive do not appear to be logical, *trust* your Teacher; remember, you are beginning a process of reorientation toward an existence that is not only beyond physical reality but also temporarily beyond your current level of understanding.

The process involves two persons, therefore both must be of the redeemed for communication to be received. To begin, open this book to the rear endpaper, upon which has been reproduced a simple diagram that provides the essentials of rudimentary communication. If you wish, you may also use a photocopy of this illustration or a legible hand-drawn facsimile of equal or larger size.[4] Remove the plastic "white stone," and place the illustration between yourself and the other person. Place the white stone roughly in the center of the diagram, with yourself and your partner each resting one or two finger tips upon the textured portion of the stone. The narrow, non-textured end will be utilized to indicate your message, therefore it should point upward, toward the top of the diagram.

---

[4]Discussed further in the Appendix.

86

Ask, "Is anyone here to speak with us?" If there is no response, wait. Be patient. If there is no response after several minutes, ask again. If still none, read your Bible while you wait, without removing your fingers from the stone. If still none, try another day; patience is a virtue, and yours will be tested.

If your stone moves of its own accord, follow the motion with your hand as your fingers continue to rest upon the stone. The first response should be to the *yes* in the upper left-hand corner; if any other initial response is received, politely but firmly move your stone to *goodbye*, then wait a few minutes and try again.

If you receive a *yes,* then say, "Please tell me your name so that I may properly address you." Your stone will then move to spell the name you are to know. Always be patient—very, very patient.

> *Beloved, do not believe every spirit, but test the spirits to see whether they are of God . . . . By this you know the Spirit of God: every spirit which confesses that Jesus Christ has come in the flesh is of God, and every spirit that does not confess Jesus is not of God.* (1 John 4:1-3)

After you receive the name, verify that the consciousness is of God by asking: "Do you confess that you are (insert name you were given) and that Jesus Christ has come in the flesh?" If you do not receive a *yes,* politely but firmly move the stone to *goodbye;* then, wait a few moments before trying to communicate again.

It should be noted that responses are always dynamic and never static; the stone must physically *move.* In other words, if it is upon the *yes* when another question is asked to which the answer is yes, the stone must actually move away from the *yes* and back again. A lack of motion always means *no answer,* and nothing more.

After you receive a yes to the confession, extend your love to your Teacher by name, for instance, "I wish you love, (name)." Or simply, "Love, (name)." It is the sincerity that counts, not flowery language. Always use simple, courteous, "plain talk." Always be reverent, and always honor your Teacher.

At this point, both you and your partner have "received" your white stones. Any further communication will depend strictly upon the role you are to play in this final drama of the age and your individual program of transfiguration.

Now ask, "Is there anything you wish me to know?" and, if he wishes to communicate further, he will tell you. When the message is complete, ask, "Is there anything further you wish me to know?"

You may ask questions concerning the messages you receive, to clarify their meaning; however, if you have questions on a subject of your own choosing, wait until your Teacher has no more for you to know. Then, if you wish, ask, "May I ask a question concerning . . . ?" If the response is *yes,* then ask your question. If it is *no,* do not. *Listen* to your Teacher, asking very few questions of your own choosing. Respect him, and honor his understanding of what you are only beginning to learn.

If you have asked a question of your own, always defer to your Teacher when you are through. Again ask, "Is there anything further you wish me to know?"

When your Teacher has no more to tell you, then say,

"Love—and goodbye," and he will move the stone to *goodbye*.

Offer to communicate with your Teacher whenever you feel moved to. Seek his direction on difficult matters. Verify understandings with him. And remember: everything he tells you, and everything he tells you to *do*, has a purpose— a purpose you will not comprehend until you have learned much, much more. Trust him, for he is your Teacher; he is sent of God to guide you, and to lead you into the Truth.

And the white stone only *begins* your ascent:

*And though the Lord give you the bread of adversity and the water of affliction, yet your Teacher will not hide himself any more, but your eyes shall see your Teacher. And your ears shall hear a word behind you, saying, "This is the way, walk in it," when you turn to the right or when you turn to the left.* (Isaiah 30:20-21)

## TWENTY-TWO

In the course of our business, my wife and I annually conduct a formal luncheon for about a thousand professional persons, most of whom are men. During the luncheon she and I are seated at a rectangular headtable that is adjacent to the speaker's lectern, both of which are uncomfortably elevated on a large dais, or raised platform. At the conclusion of the luncheon it is my practice to shakily advance upon this lectern with a large number of prepared notes (which I have always found necessary to avoid stage fright) and begin a lengthy and somewhat stilted professional presentation.

The last such event was held only a few weeks ago in the ballroom of a large hotel. The meetings were unusually special for me this year, for two of my daughters were assisting our usually meager staff. They both had been unable to arrange suitable baby sitters, however, the result of which was that their two charming children—a boy of almost two and a girl of three—were constantly and delightfully underfoot.

The night before the luncheon another dream came to me, of the type I had come to know would presage some important understanding or event. In the dream, I was with a group of people who were casually talking among themselves as they prepared to conduct a meeting of some sort. Eventually they quieted and turned to me, for I was about to speak to them as a group. I opened my mouth— but nothing came forth as my throat muscles contorted spasmodically and refused to function. Startled, I awoke; not knowing what would happen next, but knowing for certain that *something* would.

Several hours before the luncheon, I retired to the seclusion of a small room at the hotel to plan my presentation and write my speech. I sat down with pen and paper and began to write, first one line, then the next, then—nothing.

I could not write, for the muscles in my hand had suddenly contorted spasmodically and refused to function. Regardless of how hard I tried, I could not write. But I remembered the dream, and I knew that whatever it was about was soon to happen.

As the luncheon progressed, I was fully aware that I was absolutely and totally unprepared for my speech. I was unconcerned, however, for I knew I was not *supposed* to be prepared. I knew something was about to happen, and I would soon find out what it was.

Finally, the waiters began to clear the dishes—the cue for my presentation. I walked to the lectern feeling casual and carefree, for I knew from the experiences of the past few months that everything was under control. Confidently, I positioned the microphone and signalled for the houselights to be lowered; although I as yet had no idea of what I was about to say, a comforting, familiar calmness permeated my being. As my eyes swept the audience, I asked within my mind if he indeed had something planned, and my upper back was suddenly, intensely alive with his response.

The houselights dimmed, instigating a massive shuffle of chairs as the circular dining arrangements were abandoned in favor of a more comfortable view of the dais. A small child at the front of the audience, however, perceived the brief commotion as the beckoning of a sudden opportunity: unnoticed in the dimness, he slipped from his mother's lap, located an empty chair on which to stand, and unobtrusively maneuvered it to the front of the dais.

The audience quieted.

The seconds ticked by, as I waited; then, the blonde hair of my little grandson appeared over the edge of the head-table as he struggled to see his grandfather in action. I knew this was it.

I reached over the table and picked him up, holding him in my arms for all to see. I introduced him to the audience, who were mostly fathers and grandfathers themselves; the resulting applause was deafening. Then my small granddaughter came up and she, too, was introduced as a second wave of resounding applause rattled the chandeliers. I began to speak—not about the usual professional things, but about the children. Every eye was upon them, as our love for them was made evident for all to see.

After the luncheon there was no talk of business, for all the fathers were completely immersed in telling each other of their children. Their love flooded the room.

And as waves of verification surged up and down within my body, I realized that these events were actually a private, symbolic celebration of the developing fulfillment of yet another prophecy:

*Behold, I will send you Elijah the prophet before the great and terrible day of the Lord comes. And he will turn the hearts of fathers to their children and the hearts of children to their fathers, lest I come and smite the land with a curse.* (Malachi 4:5-6)[1]

Several days later, this book began to come forth. One morning, as it neared completion, I found myself idly musing upon the single, crystal-clear word that had suddenly appeared within my mind and relentlessly refused to leave. Asking its purpose, I received no response. It was a simple word, of no particular consequence, but it remained locked into my mind as though it were permanently glued in place. I reached for a sheet of paper and recorded the word, at which point it disappeared from my mind and was replaced by another equally relentless and persistent word, therefore I recorded it also. Within minutes I had received what is recorded here as the final chapter of this book—but in his words, not mine.

I have since learned that this final refinement of communication represents the primary method by which the Koran was dictated to Mohammed, the Book of Mormon to Joseph Smith, and the original scriptures of the Bible to the Lambs who have preceded me.

Now that this book is complete, I am told that I shall soon commence work on *The Second Book of the Lamb*, which will tell more of God's plan for us, more of our reality,

---

[1] The underlying allegorical meaning of this passage deals with a fundamental realization that Elijah brings to mankind wherein, as the revelation unfolds, children and adults shall perceive one another in a completely new way.

and will also begin to explain the prior words of God that have been given mankind. And it will show how Judaism, Islam, Christianity, Buddhism, and all the major theologies of earth were intentionally and lovingly given only portions of the truth—*different* portions—to make the consciousnesses of mankind search, struggle, and grow.

Children of God, it is the end of the age. Yet as it closes, a new age dawns—a very special age for those who hold fast to the will of God while growing in grace, love, and awareness.

A very special age for the next graduating class.

94

# TWENTY-THREE

*Received May 30, 1984*

*Behold, I have caused the words of this book to be written by the hand of my Lamb, and then to be sealed in Heaven even as they have been sealed on earth. He is my firstborn, my righteous one, my servant in whom God is well pleased. He is Elijah. He is a Root of David, even as I myself am and even as is he who came before me. He is my appointed messenger on earth, and it is decreed that he continue to write and preach unto the divulging of all that has been promised from of old and even all that has been hidden from you, the existence of which you knew not.*

*Behold, the ark of the covenant is come.*

*I am coming. I am the Holy Ghost. I am Messiah. I am Christ. I have loved, nurtured, forged, and reprimanded you for two thousand years, by the authority of the one God who created all, even me and those who came before me. And now I gather the fruits of my labor, my beloved redeemed of the earth, and commence to transfigure them, which I am accomplishing even now. Their judgment has been decreed.*

*To those who have conquered, I say, "Welcome to the overflowing love of your God and those who have conquered before you." To those who have not conquered, I say, "Always love, always do God's will, and you too will conquer, for it is so ordained." To those who refuse God's will, I say, "Your judgment is also decreed."*

*I give to my redeemed—those who have received the white stone—a symbol, which I have caused to be at the front of this book, so that you may know one another. The symbol is to be used by no other persons, neither is it to have made of it any material thing, but it is to be used only as a mark.*

*And to my redeemed I also give a commandment: that you earnestly and reverently seek the instruction of Heaven in the ways I have provided, for by this you will be transfigured.*

*I am coming, in overflowing love, to take you home.*

# AFTERWORD

The development of this book, and the events relating thereto, has been an unusual and bizarre experience for one accustomed only to the hard facts of reality. Not being previously of any particular theological persuasion, however, I found it delightful to find—at long last—something that finally felt *right*, deep down inside.

And indeed it is. For as circumstances have progressed beyond the experiences recorded herein, so has the volume of information literally exploded in quantity. The communication methods described, you see, represented a continuum of development—starting with the white stone, through internal thought processes and verification protocols, and then to the level represented by Chapter 23: word-for-word dictation directly from the Holy Ghost.

But he did not stop there; shortly after the completion of this book, I began receiving what ultimately amounted to over eighty essays, each dictated word for word directly from Above. They further describe the nature of our reality, the Sons of God, Heaven, and the basis or thought processes behind the development of earth's school of mankind. They describe more of the reasoning behind the scriptures of all lands, and furthermore tell of the growth of consciousness—how it works, and why. These essays, received within approximately two months, form *The Second Book of the Lamb.*

It is an incredible work, and it is already complete—for you to read, digest, and from which to form your own opinions. In so doing, you will share my delight as you personally experience the unbounded intellect and nurturing ways of the Master Schoolteacher himself.

It's been almost a year now, since it all began. If I hadn't experienced it first-hand, I myself could not have initially believed what was transpiring. But now I *know* it is real—all of it—for I've seen too much evidence now. And there is more coming, already. Much more.

Peter C. Stone
September 26, 1984

*My teaching is not mine, but His who sent me; if any man's will is to do His will, he shall know whether the teaching is from God or whether I am speaking on my own authority. He who speaks on his own authority seeks his own glory; but he who seeks the glory of Him who sent him is true, and in him there is no falsehood.*

—John 7:16-18

# APPENDIX

## The Implements of Communication

The white stone is used with a simple diagram consisting of the words *yes, no,* and *goodbye,* the numerals *0* through *9,* and the characters of the alphabet *A* through *Z*. I prefer to also add a "happy face"; while not essential, it is a pleasant universal symbol that will be used often. The resulting diagram will be found reproduced on the rear endpaper of this book, together with a removable, plastic "white stone." Please refer to Chapter 21 for detailed instructions regarding their use.

Should the diagram at the rear of this book prove too small for convenient use, an enlarged facsimile may be drawn by hand on an ordinary sheet of white typing paper. In so doing, use large, uniform characters with ample space between them, such that the white stone may indicate your message without ambiguity. A hand-drawn facsimile should also be prepared by those who wish to employ a language other than English, substituting however the correct words and alphabet of their native tongue. Hand-drawn diagrams should be as neat and legible as possible, not only because they are to serve the practical purpose of communication, but also as a gesture of sincerity and respect for those with whom you will communicate.

If you have already established an on-going communicative relationship with a specific Teacher, you may occasionally find yourself in a situation where your communication diagram is at home and you have a simple question to ask, such as, "Should I do thus and so?" In such an event, you need merely sketch the words *yes* and *no* on a scrap of paper, open the communicative interchange as you would at home, and then simply ask your question! You will be taught more of these techniques by your Teacher.

Should your plastic "white stone" be misplaced, a substitute may likewise be fabricated of available materials—any small white object of low friction will suffice, such as a white guitar pick, a large white button, or a triangle cut from the back of a white business card.

Larger fingers may also require larger "stones," which may then require larger communication diagrams to avoid ambiguity. In such an event, simply fabricate what you need; it need only be neat, legible, and functional.

*This earth, in its sanctified and immortal state, will be made like unto crystal and will be a Urim and Thummim to the inhabitants who dwell thereon, whereby all things pertaining to an inferior kingdom, or all kingdoms of a lower order, will be manifest to those who dwell on it; and this earth will be Christ's.*

*Then the white stone mentioned in Revelation 2:17, will become a Urim and Thummim to each individual who receives one, whereby things pertaining to a higher order of kingdoms will be made known;*

*And a white stone is given to each of those who come into the celestial kingdom, whereon is a new name written, which no man knoweth save he that receiveth it. The new name is the key word.*[1]

—Joseph Smith, April 2, 1843

[1]*Doctrine and Covenants,* Church of Jesus Christ of Latter-day Saints, Section 130:9-11.

*Then I looked, and lo, a white cloud, and seated on the cloud one like a son of man, with a golden crown on his head, and a sharp sickle in his hand. And another angel came out of the temple, calling with a loud voice to him who sat upon the cloud, "Put in your sickle, and reap, for the hour to reap has come, for the harvest of the earth is fully ripe." So he who sat upon the cloud swung his sickle on the earth, and the earth was reaped.*

—Revelation 14:14-16

# INDEX

Yes 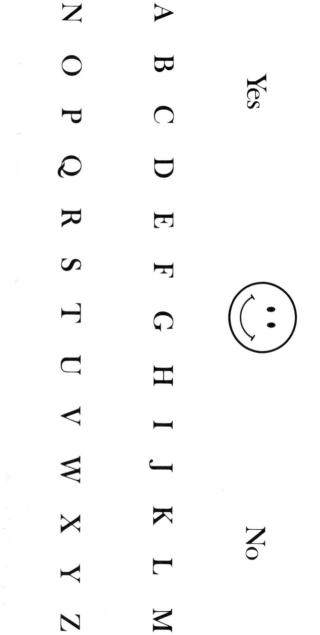 No

A B C D E F G H I J K L M

N O P Q R S T U V W X Y Z

Goodbye 0 1 2 3 4 5 6 7 8 9